IGNITE YOUR CREATIVE SPARK

20 Ways to Fire up Your Imagination

JORDAN AYAN

In the new millennium, we face a level of challenge and opportunity that exceeds anything in the history of man. Fortunately, we have the ability to deal with this new world because we have the ability to be innovative and creative. The key is for each of us to understand the incredible creative power we possess, and know how to fuel that power with inspiration. This guide is designed to provide the reader with a new level of creative understanding and to introduce some easy-to-use tools that will inspire new vistas of creative exploration.

Graphics by Balance Design

COLOR
YOURSELF
CREATIVE

Are you in the habit of thinking you're not creative? If so, it's time to abandon that myth. You are innately creative, and you've always been! You just need to rekindle your natural creative spirit.

Remember when you were in grade school? Think about the unbridled creative energy and abundant curiosity surging in you back then. You could turn a box of wooden blocks into a city, a lump of clay into a dinosaur, and a throwaway cardboard box into a special hideaway. If you were like I was, one of your real favorites was a giant box of 64 crayons. You could capture the world with your rainbow of colors. You could let your imagination soar without limits.

Unfortunately, somewhere along the way, in the process of "growing-up" and learning the "rules," you abandoned your box of colors. You gave in to the myth of thinking that as an adult, you must hide your creative instincts and instead conform to the tried-and-true path. You exchanged your 64 crayons for a 29-cent ballpoint pen.

Don't let the myths continue to stifle your spark and quash your big ideas. It's time to stop that inner critic murmuring in your ear, "Oh, you're just not the creative type," or "You don't have any creative talent." Such unconscious thinking signals your brain that it's fine to let other people do the creative work.

Destroy the myths that block your creativity. Once you begin flexing your creative muscle, you'll find yourself once again producing a rainbow of big ideas.

> "THERE'S NO SHORTAGE OF IDEAS IN LIFE,
>
> JUST A SHORTAGE OF PEOPLE WHO RECOGNIZE THEM."
>
> J. Peterman, *Catalog entrepreneur*

Creativity is a lifelong process. You don't just sit down and say, "Now I am going to be creative and have a great idea." Creativity takes time. Ideas must form and foment in your mind. There are tools and techniques that you can use to improve your ability to generate ideas. There are four that I consider the most vital. They form what I call your creative C.O.R.E.®:

Curiosity: You must have a burning desire to know about the world and everything in it. Your curiosity drives you to wonder if something in your life can be done differently or improved.

Openness to people and ideas: You must be willing to accept people and ideas that differ from your own background. Your openness allows you to explore new paths and diverse opinions, which lead to new ideas.

Risk Tolerance: You must walk through life unafraid to take a risk now and then. Your ability to tolerate risk may put you out on the edge once in a while, but that's where the newest ideas and biggest payoffs are.

Energy: You must maintain a boundless energy for life, for helping others, and for making yourself a better thinker. Your energy keeps your mind constantly moving and thinking.

Invest in your creative C.O.R.E.® Take time every day to encourage your personal creative exploration. Investigate something new that you find interesting, listen to a new style of music, or talk to someone whose perspective is different from your own. Over time, you will find that your creative juices will flow with increasing ease and enjoyment. You may even discover that great idea or come face to face with your next profitable business opportunity.

DEVELOP YOUR
CREATIVE
C.O.R.E.®

TAP YOUR CREATIVE
SOUL

"OUR IMAGINATION IS OUR PREVIEW
OF COMING ATTRACTIONS." Albert Einstein

New ideas have their roots deep in your creative soul. How can you bring them forth? What process can you use to encourage your creativity to soar?

The model that has become the most accepted method of tapping into your creative soul was developed in the late nineteenth century. This model is based on defining creativity as a four-step process.

1. Preparation During this stage, you firm up your understanding of your problem or opportunity, and then set out to gather information, resources, or research to solve it. In many ways, all life is preparation for creativity.

2. Incubation During this phase, you take no conscious action toward solving your dilemma. Simply let your mind work on its own, behind the scenes. Let your unconscious mind take over and play with the information, making its own connections.

3. Illumination This is the famous moment where your Aha! occurs. Your unconscious mind has worked the information and discovered the solution. You can't force this point. It is likely to present itself when you are relaxed and least expecting it. But when it happens, make sure you capture it immediately.

4. Implementation After an idea presents itself, the real proof is in the doing. Implementation is when the rubber meets the road and the idea is put into action. This is when you refine and polish your idea, and get others to adopt it.

So, take the steps now to tap into your creative soul.

> "BELIEF CONSISTS IN ACCEPTING
> THE AFFIRMATIONS OF THE SOUL; UNBELIEF IN
> DENYING THEM." Ralph Waldo Emerson

A few years ago, researchers did an experiment to measure creativity and discovered a striking trend. Their research indicated that ideas developed by children under the age of five were deemed to be "original" nearly 90 percent of the time. By age seven though, the percentage of ideas considered original dropped to 20 percent. The worst news was that only 2 percent of adult's ideas could be classified as original. This experiment raises the question: Are adults less creative in their thinking than children?

The answer is a resounding "no." Adults often simply stop believing in their creative abilities. For whatever reason, adults abandon their childhood creative genius and accept less originality in their life.

The problem is, belief in your own creative abilities and energies has a tremendous impact on your ability to generate ideas. The mind moves in the direction of its dominant thoughts, and so failing to believe in your own creative power only leads to its own demise. The next time your inner critic tells you "you're not creative," or you hear feedback from others telling you to give up your creative thinking, don't accept those words.

Just as simple belief is all it took to bring Tinkerbell back to life in the classic story, Peter Pan, your own positive thinking will bring creativity back to your life.

"I believe in my own creativity" is a powerful phrase. Try it today.

DO YOU BELIEVE?

THERE IS NO SUCH THING AS A STUPID QUESTION

If there is one way to increase your creative ability, it is learning to ask questions. Why, you ask? (You see, you're already off to a good start.) Because questions are one of life's greatest creative tools. They allow you to endlessly learn.

The universe of what we don't know is always expanding. By the time we are adults, most of us have a natural tendency to think that we have the answers to most questions we face in life. But in reality, the universe of knowledge is so vast that we cannot even be aware of what we don't know. And since there is always something new, what we are unaware of knowing actually keeps growing.

This means that the only way you can come close to knowing what you don't know is to keep asking questions. Little by little, question by question, you will get closer to the edge of the universe. You will never really get there, but that's the fun of life, the creative challenge.

Children instinctively understand this dilemma. They never stop asking questions, but they constantly enjoy learning something new. They are curious without embarrassment. Nothing stops children from wanting to know, until they are made to feel that it's wrong to ask questions. Then they lose their curiosity. Did that happen to you? Did you learn to fear asking questions, as if your curiosity was a sign of weakness? The next time you want to ask a question, do it. Your lack of knowledge is your greatest opportunity, a sign of your creative genius.

"THE MAN WHO DOES NOT READ

GOOD BOOKS HAS NO ADVANTAGE OVER THE MAN

WHO CAN'T READ THEM." Mark Twain

Have you considered the amazing power of the written word? It allows you to see what you cannot visit, experience what you cannot feel, and touch what you cannot imagine. Reading sows the seeds of your future success. As you read, you stimulate your mind to make new connections and associations, and those fresh thoughts can be the kindling for many a creative endeavor.

Most of us tend to be too narrow in our reading habits, devotedly and unvaryingly reading the same kinds of materials. To challenge your mind, broaden your reading repertoire. Go beyond the trade magazines in your industry and your local newspaper. Why not pick up the trades from a totally unrelated field or buy a newspaper from another city or even a foreign country? Next time you visit a bookstore or library, go to an unfamiliar section and browse books unrelated to your current interests. You may well stumble upon a solution to a problem that's had you stymied.

To ignite your ideas, expand the scope of what you read. Buckminster Fuller, one of the 20th century's most prolific inventors and thinkers, devised a clever way to make sure he always had fresh food for thought. Whenever he visited a newsstand, he unfailingly purchased and read whatever magazine or paper was shelved in the upper right hand corner of the rack. Over the years, this strategy fed his mind all manner of unexpected ideas and opinions from beyond the boundaries of his normal workday life.

STRETCH YOUR
READING ROUTINE

COLLABORATING
CREATES
BREAKTHROUGHS

Winning ideas often become so because they are fueled by the power of collaboration. History is filled with the results of wonderful successful creative collaborations. Consider the Wright Brothers, Rogers and Hammerstein, Apple Computer's Wozniak and Jobs, or Hewlett and Packard. This doesn't mean you need to form committees every time you want to be creative. But having a collaborative team available to you that can come together at the right moment can help you develop and strengthen your ideas. Teams are especially valuable in business situations, where they can dramatically improve the chances of an idea's success in the world.

One of the best ways to collaborate is to build a large network of people to whom you can go for guidance, suggestions, and feedback. Build your network out of a broad range of people: business associates, colleagues, customers, friends, and even well-known professionals in your field and others. It's possible to reach anyone in the world if you really try.

Once you build your network, the key to a successful collaboration is to be completely willing to open your ideas to others. Don't protect "your" ideas so tightly that you suffocate them. Share them around, and willingly invite others to help you make them better, wiser, and more creative.

Remember also to reciprocate. Offer your services and feedback to everyone in your network who requests help. You will find that whatever support you give others will come back to you when you need it. That's the power of networks.

"THE WORLD IS A BOOK, AND THOSE WHO
DO NOT TRAVEL READ ONLY A PAGE." St. Augustine

Need a dose of inspiration? Try hitting the road. Travel can be a tremendous source of new ideas. It upgrades our "cultural software."

The reason is quite simple. We all live within our minds. Our upbringing and daily environment determine our philosophy of life. We look at the world each day, and tend to see only our own point of view. Most importantly, whenever we face an issue that requires problem solving or decision making, our mind automatically loads up our usual cultural software which becomes our operating system. We are not even aware that there may be other operating systems in the world.

Traveling introduces you to other operating systems. When you visit different cities, states, and especially other countries, you begin to see that there are many lifestyles, customs, habits, and philosophies – and that no single one is the "right" way to live. As you open your mind to new experiences and perspectives, your cultural programming will begin to expand, and seed you with new beliefs, attitudes, and ideas.

To increase your creative spark, expand your horizons whenever you are out of town. Even a single day business trip can lead to a wealth of experiences that might fuel your creativity. Whenever you can, go outside of your comfort zone to be an explorer. Use your natural curiosity to find out about something different when you are in a new location. Strike up a conversation with a few of the "natives." Avoid the tendency to eat and shop in chain restaurants and stores that might as well be a block from your house. Explore something new, something you don't know. With just a bit of effort you can be traveling to new ideas in no time.

GO TO WHERE THE IDEAS ARE

A WORLD WIDE WEB
OF IDEA POWER

When the history books are written about the 20th century, there is no doubt that computer technology will be at the top of the critical contributions of our time. Computers radically changed the world in the same way that hand tools changed the world during the Industrial Revolution. The creation of the microchip has added a new level to the power and ability of machines to do tasks that formerly required painstaking time and effort.

From a creative perspective, one byproduct of computer technology that has brought us to the dawn of a new idea renaissance is the World Wide Web. Never in history have so many people been able to connect so easily with others to share interests and creatively collaborate. The Web does for humanity's ideas what the chip did for machines. With a simple phone connection and computer, anyone can have access to the entire wealth of humankind's knowledge through the ages.

How's your technology quotient? If you are not yet hooked up to the World Wide Web, it's time to do so. There can be no excuse. The Web will allow you to take advantage of our era's most powerful creative tool. You can learn about almost anything you ever wanted to know, and you can contact millions of people who might change your life.

To keep your ideas flowing in the future, tune in to the Web. This new technology will take your creative process into the 21st century.

"IDEAS ARE THE BEGINNING POINT OF ALL FORTUNES." Napoleon Hill

How often has seeing a new product or idea caused you to mutter, "I thought of that months ago, but I had completely forgotten it."

Most of us have ideas continuously flowing through our heads, but because our ideas are nebulous and unformed, we ignore, or worse, squelch them. It would be silly to suggest that you should develop every idea that occurs to you. You can, however, enhance your creative success by mastering the art of "idea capture."

If you make a conscientious effort to record, collect, and save your ideas as they come to you, you can stave off creative bankruptcy.

Idea capture is a well-practiced habit among history's most creative people. Such paragons of creativity as Leonardo Da Vinci, Benjamin Franklin, and Thomas Edison perfected the process of collecting their ideas. They literally made an art form of it.

Don't forfeit your thoughts. Always be prepared to record your emergent notions.

Simply put, whenever you have an idea, even if you know you're in no position to do anything about it, you should capture it. Write it in a notebook, enter it into a computer file, or dictate it into a pocket recorder. Build an idea journal, and it will feed your future success.

Keep in mind that, once an idea pops into your head, you have only about ten minutes within which to capture it, and if you take no steps to save it, your idea is likely to be gone forever.

CATCH YOUR IDEAS

BEFORE THEY'RE GONE

THE FOUR P's OF CREATIVE SUCCESS

"THE WORLD CAN ONLY BE GRASPED BY ACTION,

NOT BY CONTEMPLATION... THE HAND IS THE CUTTING

EDGE OF THE MIND." Jacob Bronowski

Ideas without action are just idle thoughts. No one has ever been successful or built a business from idle thoughts. The key to creative success is being able to take an idea all the way through the process, from initial concept to implementation.

How can you do this? In my view, there are four critical components to making your ideas more than idle thoughts. I call these components the four P's of creative success.

Planning: Once they have an idea, creative individuals are often weak when it comes to planning and setting goals for their ideas. If you want to make an idea happen, you have to scope out a plan for its success. Writing your plan is best.

Persistence: Whenever researchers look into the characteristics of individuals who are successfully creative, persistence stands out on top. No matter how great your concept, you will encounter idea killers and naysayers who can find every reason to portray your idea negatively. To make your idea happen, you have to stick with it for months, years, even decades.

Passion: When everyone and everything is stacked against your idea, your personal zeal can often keep it alive. You'll see that being passionate about your idea is contagious.

Patience: Persistence and patience go hand in hand. Success seldom happens on your timetable. In fact, it is likely that you will need to wait for just the right moment when the rest of the world catches up to your great idea.

Pursue this process with your ideas to make them more than idle thoughts!

"The pessimist sees difficulty in every opportunity. The optimist sees the opportunity in every difficulty." Winston Churchill

Do you encourage people to develop their ideas? The single greatest loss to businesses today is new thinking that never gets implemented because it is stopped by a poisonous environment that kills ideas before they are developed. Most organizations are filled with people who seem determined to kill the ideas of others. Sit through any meeting, and listen to the ugly sounds that occur as new ideas pop up. Every company has its favorites, but they usually sound something like:

"It's not in the budget."
"We've tried that before."
"That'll never work."
"The customer will never accept that."
"Let's forget you even said that."

Whatever the phrase, the impact is always the same. It stops ideas cold, but more importantly, it has a much more devastating impact of stopping the flow of inspiration.

To create an environment where ideas are welcomed, take steps to eliminate killer phrases in your work. Have your team determine the most common idea killers in the company, and then institute a policy that fines anyone for the use of those phrases at meetings. As many a successful company will tell you, even the most insane idea can turn out to be the goldmine you've been looking for.

STOP IDEA KILLERS BEFORE THEY STOP YOU

CHALLENGE
YOUR
ASSUMPTIONS

> "THE THINKING THAT HAS BROUGHT ME
> THIS FAR HAS CREATED SOME PROBLEMS THAT
> THIS THINKING CAN'T SOLVE." Albert Einstein

Do you often become blinded by the status quo when you face a problem or new challenge? Do you find comfort in doing things the way they have always been done? Do you have a "usual" way of doing things?

I call this kind of attitude "assumptive thinking," because you assume away your best ideas without giving them a chance. You assume a solution won't work; you assume other people won't support you; you assume your boss will say "No;" you assume – you assume – you assume. Assumptive thinking stops you from seeing the really creative solutions that exist. Go beyond assumptive thinking. Identify your assumptions and then challenge them. Follow this process:

1. Develop a clear statement of your problem or opportunity, and put this statement in writing.

2. Brainstorm a list of any assumptions you are making about the situation described in the problem statement. For example, if your problem statement is, "In what ways can we improve mail delivery?" an appropriate assumption might be that mail even has to be delivered. As long as you are focused on improving mail delivery, you are limiting your options.

3. Reexamine your problem statement to see if there is a way to restate it without the assumptions. In the mail example, the problem might be restated, "In what way can we best bring people and their mail together." This problem statement will allow you to identify many more creative solutions than the first statement.

Take time to challenge assumptions when you are searching for creative opportunities. Your best ideas may be masked by your definition of the problem.

Have you ever noticed how eager you are to stomp on a new idea? In corporate America, the average life span of a new idea is no more than ten seconds. Once a fledgling idea is announced, there's always someone ready to squash it, claiming it won't work or that it's flawed.

If your organization is like this, it's time to make a change. Get rid of that arsenal of idea-killer phrases people use like hand grenades, demolishing infant ideas before they've had a chance to take form. Replace such weaponry with an attitude of open exploration. Don't judge ideas until you've fully considered them. Even seemingly ludicrous ideas may contain components of greatness.

A group of engineers at NASA have implemented an idea-inviting technique. Their approach, dubbed PINS, ensures that every idea gets a fair shake. They realized that whenever they considered a new idea, their natural inclination was to focus on the negative aspects. To control this tendency, the PINS process was applied. It requires each engineer to devote equal time to answering four questions:

P – Positive What do I think are the worthwhile aspects of this idea?
I – Interesting What aspects do I find interesting or which have merit for me?
N – Negative What do I consider the unworkable aspects of this idea?
S – Suggestions What can I add or suggest that will make this a better idea?

Of course, the PINS process works two ways. First, the next time you have the urge to trample someone's idea, hold your breath. Similarly, the next time you want to share your own brainstorms, ask your colleagues to give your ideas breathing space, too. There's a world of unimagined possibilities out there.

GIVE YOUR IDEAS
BREATHING
SPACE

ARE YOU HAVING FUN YET?

Jerry Greenfield, *Co-founder of Ben & Jerry's*

Too many of us forget to do the most important thing in life as we mature into adulthood: have fun. When you take life or yourself too seriously, you end up stressed and uptight, a state that does not allow the subconscious to explore and your ideas to flow.

Fun is a great creativity enhancer. Sometimes the best thing you can do to get your mind thinking creatively is to relax, laugh, and enjoy yourself. Adding fun to any situation can be as easy as sharing a joke, playing a game, or going to an amusement park. The key is to figure out what is fun for you, and then to make a point to do it more often. What counts is finding a way to let your "child" out.

If you really want to learn to have fun, spend some quality time with children. Read to them – or even better – make up your own stories. Play a board game, cut out paper dolls, or fashion a tent out of two chairs and a sheet and allow yourself to be drawn into their games of imagination and fantasy. See the world from their musings. You will quickly fall back into your childhood and re-experience true creativity.

If you think you don't have the time, it proves you need to make the time. The attitude of thinking you don't have the time for fun is exactly why you need to take time to have fun. So, the next time you find yourself at a stuffy meeting, let everyone know, "kidding is encouraged!"

You've probably heard of "brainstorming." Most organizations these days encourage their teams to brainstorm together to generate new ideas and products. Brainstorming is effective because it helps the participants take advantage of multiple minds all focused on the same problem together.

To get a team to truly optimize their creative work and to stimulate new ideas, you need to apply "PowerThinking" techniques. PowerThinking techniques are based on getting your group to go outside of their normal "thinking box" by providing an outside stimulus that triggers truly new viewpoints.

Following are two types of effective power thinking technique:

Words – Introduce a set of random words from the dictionary to your group. As you share each random word, ask your group to think how that word might suggest solutions to your problem. You will be astonished at the wild but interesting links people can make between a word and the problem or opportunity you are discussing.

Pictures – Try using random pictures clipped from magazines and catalogues. (As they say, a picture is worth a thousand words.) See what novel ideas the pictures suggest.

PowerThinking techniques are simple, but they work. Your team may find them a bit awkward at first, but with practice, they will be generating so many new ideas that go beyond what you would get from traditional brainstorming.

POWER
THINK
OUT OF YOUR BOX

FASHION YOURSELF A CREATIVE PLACE

> "NECESSITY MAY BE THE MOTHER OF INVENTION, BUT CURIOSITY IS THE MOTHER OF DISCOVERY." Charles Handy

Where do you have your best ideas? Most people have a special place where their ideas seem to flow more freely. In many cases, it's a room or location where they can feel relaxed, unpressured, and open to inspiration.

There's actually a good reason behind this phenomenon. When your mind is relaxed, it gives your subconscious free reign to sift through the hodge-podge of ideas and images floating within, and make "connections" between them. These unexpected links often become the inspiration for a new idea.

Well, why not arrange to have a creative place in your office where people can go to relax and daydream? Why not outfit one of your conference rooms or offices with couches, easy chairs, lamps, artwork, maybe even some games and toys. Sure, people can do paperwork and toss around new ideas while sitting in a cramped office, and they can get work done in a stuffy conference room, but neither location is going to get their real creative juices flowing.

Look around the building where you work. Are the walls blank? Modify a room or carve out a place where your people can loosen up and shirk off the pressures of the day. It could be as simple as adding some color, energizing artwork, plants, or music to your creative space.

One company, Lucent Technologies, takes this concept so seriously that they created an entire room called Ideaverse, filled with comfortable bean bag chairs, murals, music, and a wide assortment of toys to stimulate the mind. Lucent teams use the facility whenever they are trying to merge their creative spirit with their technological brilliance.

Many teams working on finding a new idea tend to stop fairly early in their brainstorming or thinking process. The typical team may generate twenty or thirty ideas, breathe a collective sigh of relief, and conclude that they have gone about as far as they can in developing a solution. Not wanting to beat a dead horse, they pick one of those ideas and call it a day.

That's all well and good, but did you know that if you want to increase your chances of finding the greatest ideas, you need to keep pushing beyond the normal point of stopping? It's been shown that teams who are willing to persist find that real breakthrough ideas often come later in an idea development session when they really have to stretch.

So, the next time you are in a group, watch the dynamics of your interactions. You will notice that your group will tend to have a natural stopping point, marked by a lull in the action. This is the point where many teams think they have exhausted all their ideas and so they wrap it up and select one of the earlier candidates. But this is exactly the point at which you should dig in and work harder to get an even larger volume of ideas. It may seem that the suggestions and ideas start to get ridiculous at this point, but from the seeds of these wild things grow the really interesting options.

So, don't halt the thinking when you think you've exhausted the well. Crank up your creative output and you'll be rewarded with the real gems.

CRANK UP THE CREATIVE VOLUME

TUNE INTO
SYNCHRONICITY

One of the most powerful resources for creative people is synchronicity. Synchronicity refers to that random fortunate meeting or event that turns out to offer the key to solving your current endeavor. It is running into someone you haven't seen in years who offers you the perfect opportunity for your idea. It is meeting a stranger who happens to know exactly the piece of information that answers your question. It is browsing through a bookstore and chancing upon a book that gets you unstuck. It is those occasions when we literally bump into an idea.

Synchronicity reminds me of that childhood game where you had to look at a picture and find hidden objects. You often could not see them until someone told you they were there. Often the ideas will just be waiting for you to see them.

Synchronicity can happen to all of us, but you have to be open to it. It often presents itself to you, but you fail to see it or take advantage of it. If you want to increase your creativity quotient, begin paying close attention to the events and people around you. Heighten your awareness of your surroundings, and take note of the direction your life seems to be leading (or pulling) you. Creative opportunities lie in every person you meet and any ideas you come across.

Being in the right place at the right time is no coincidence. Some of the best ideas are right in front of you. All you have to do is see them.

"THE ONLY SURE WAY TO AVOID MAKING
MISTAKES IS TO HAVE NO NEW IDEAS." Albert Einstein

Organizations often try to encourage their employees to contribute ideas using a formal suggestion process, including cash or gifts as rewards. While such programs seem healthy and generous, the formal suggestion process usually adds a level of complexity in its rules and regulations that kills many ideas before they see the light of day. When employees offer suggestions but don't make it to an award level, they often stop contributing. It's not because they don't have new ideas; they simply become disheartened.

Let employees know that you are eager for results – and everyone can share the rewards.

A proven strategy often used in Japanese firms is the *Kaizen*, or continuous improvement. Firms that have adopted Kaizen make it the responsibility of every employee to constantly develop ideas and methods that might improve on the work they are doing. The focus is on action, not on rewards. No idea is too small, or unappreciated. If an idea improves a process, it gets put into action, quickly.

So encourage everyone in your organization to share their ideas, then help put them into practice. By shifting the focus away from rewards and onto improvement, you'll find that the ideas will probably flow, and people will feel more positive about their contribution to the overall success of your venture.

RESULTS
NOT REWARDS

W hat is a moment of inspiration worth? No doubt it would be difficult to put a price tag on the products, services, works of art, pieces of music or written words that have graced our lives as a result of a single moment of inspiration. The main goal of this book is to provide the reader with some key ways to "ignite their creative spark," by creating more moments of inspiration.

If you want to be successful with the tools outlined in these short chapters, jot some notes to yourself in the margins on exactly how you plan to take action in each of the different topic areas. My experience in working with thousands of individuals with these tools is that every person can increase their creative output, but it requires a strong commitment to putting these techniques into practice.

As you apply these tools in your life and business, the moments of inspiration will lead to concrete ideas if you put them into action. I would appreciate learning what tools worked for you. Please e-mail me about your creative successes at jordan@create-it.com (or write to the address on the following page).

JORDAN AYAN

Jordan Ayan helps people and organizations succeed. He shows people how they can use creativity and technology in their own careers to get ahead faster, produce better results and enjoy work more than ever before. His qualifications stem from a unique background:

Successful Business Person – Jordan created a highly profitable business unit for Dun & Bradstreet by combining innovative ideas with state-of-the-art technology to develop a leading on-line service.

Successful Entrepreneur – Jordan leads his own Chicago-based consulting and training firm, *Create-It! Inc.*, which helps a wide range of organizations improve performance by leveraging innovation and technology.

Keynote Speaker – Jordan speaks around the world to best-of-class organizations and across a diverse range of industries at conventions and sales meetings to leading organizations such as Lucent Technologies, INC. Magazine, and Lockheed-Martin.

Business Advisor – Dozens of leading organizations, including Andersen Consulting, Kimberly Clark and Sprint, have used Jordan's powerful ideas and techniques for enhancing creativity and leveraging technology.

Author – Jordan's articles have appeared in numerous well-known publications. He also wrote *Aha! 10 Ways to Free Your Creative Spirit and Find Your Great Ideas,* a popular guide to fueling innovation and finding great ideas, which earned Jordan recognition on Tom Peter's list of Cool People With Hot Ideas. To purchase a copy of Aha!, visit www.create-it.com or your local bookstore.

For more information or to have Jordan speak to your organization, please contact Create-It! at:
Create-It! Inc.
2603 S.Washington Suite 140
Naperville, IL 60565

Or on the web at: www.create-it.com

Or e-mail Jordan at: Jordan@create-it.com

C.O.R.E.® and Create-It!® are registered trademarks of Create-It! Inc.

The cost is low...
but the ideas are priceless!

Share these books with your entire organization and watch the power of your team grow!

Each title in the Successories "Power of One" library takes less than 30 minutes to read, but the wisdom they contain will last a lifetime. Take advantage of volume pricing as you share these insights with all the people who impact your career, your business and your life.

Anatomy of A Leader
Carl Mays
This body of knowledge can help everyone develop the qualities of a leader. #NF713259

Attitude: Your Internal Compass
Denis Waitley and Boyd Matheson
These practical insights will help managers and employees maintain a positive outlook each day. #NF713193

Burn Brightly Without Burning Out
Dick Biggs
Boost morale and productivity by helping people balance the work they do with the life they lead. #NF716016

Companies Don't Succeed... People Do
Mac Anderson
Learn to develop employees and a recognition culture within any organization. #NF716015

Dare to Soar
Byrd Baggett
The spirit of eagles inspired this unique collection of motivational thoughts. #NF716006

The Employee Connection
Jim Harris
Learn to empower your people through open communication with these valuable tips. #NF716018

Empowerment
Ken Blanchard and Susan Fowler Woodring
Use these valuable ideas to achieve "Peak Performance Through Self-Leadership." #NF716022

Fall In Love with Your Future
Ron and Mary Beshear
Apply the principles outlined in this refreshing book and begin to take control of your future. #NF716026

Goals
Gary Ryan Blair
A refreshing mix of insights and thought-provoking exercises make this a "Guideline for Designing an Extraordinary Life." #NF716025

Ignite Your Creative Spark
Jordan Ayan
This book will reveal your hidden potential as it inspires new vistas of creative exploration. #NF716023

Motivating Today's Employees
Bob Nelson
Use this book to understand the impact of employee rewards and recognition. #NF716007

Motivating Yourself
Mac Anderson
This unique mix of proven ideas and motivating stories will help "Recharge the Human Battery." #NF716021

Motivation, Lombardi Style
Vince Lombardi
Inspire your team with these insights about the athletic playing field and the business battlefield. #NF716013

Priorities
Peggy Anderson
Learn about what it takes to "Make a Difference in the Life of a Child" and share it with others. #NF716027

The Psychology of Winning for the 21st Century
Dr. Denis Waitley
Dr. Denis Waitley provides a unique perspective on what it means to win in the 21st Century. #NF716024

Pulling Together
John Murphy
Share "The 17 Principles of Effective Teamwork" with every member of any team. #NF716019

Quality, Service, Teamwork
This valuable resource includes over 100 motivational quotes on various topics. #NF716014

Results
Jeff Blackman
Help your sales team turn passion into profit with these "Proven Strategies for Changing Times." #NF716017

Rule #One
C. Leslie Charles
There are common sense tips and easy-to-apply rules in this customer service handbook. #NF716008

Teamwork
Glenn Parker
This is a valuable blueprint for successful team building. Put it to work for your team. #NF716012

Think Change
John Murphy
This provocative commentary is designed to change people's thinking—"To Adapt and Thrive or Fall Behind." #NF716020

We've Got to Start Meeting Like This
Ron Fry
Learn to reach for results and get more out of your team meetings with these insightful tips. #NF716028

Everything You Need to Know to Get Everything You Want
Robert Stuberg
Your view of yourself and the world around you will change as you discover and apply these "Life Secrets for Success." #NF716029

Heartpower
Jim Harris, Ph.D.
This valuable advice is intended to "Get Your People to Love Your Company." #NF716030